BLACKMAN

In all we do, we do not see life
The rose of life
The beauty of life
Our future
Our God given right
It is hope
It is truth
The truth of life

Michelle Jean

To be honest with you I don't even know why I wrote this book. It seems like this book is out of the ordinary and I truly don't want to do it. I am so not into it but its written and I so don't want to go back nor do I want to go forward in editing it. Oh well here we go. And no I so do not find enthusiasm in this book.

In all I see and know, I see suffering and pain, lies told to nations to bring them closer to hell, live in more pain.

In all I see and know, I see wicked and evil strive, destroy in the name and names of their gods – false hope – lies.

In all I see and know, I see humanity feasting on the blood of the innocent, sacrificing them to death – their false gods of deceit.

I see the web of lies – yes the world wide web of governments, religion, social media, individuals themselves.

Ah yes blood and human sacrifices are nothing new because they were and still are a part of the Babylonian way of life; our modern day system of things, our religious system of lies and deceit. All that which is religion hath to do with blood and human sacrifices onto the dead of hell.

In all I see and know, I know God – Good God. I also know death hence I tell you all that I see and know.

I am not here to lie to you nor am I here to die for you. In all that I do I tell you the truth and although my books are filled with errors and typos it cannot be helped as I do not have an editor nor do I want or need one. Know that I've tried my best to make these books error free given my present state but failed. So please forgive me because I've learnt when Good God tell you to do something, you cannot bring someone else in the picture to add or take away from that which was told and given truthfully to you.

You are to keep the word of God – Good God come what may.

Truth is, good life is given to all, but it is not all that want a good life.

You need to know that if you are unclean you cannot reside with Good God. You can only reside with death and truth be known, not even death want some of us because some of us condemn death, meaning make death truly unclean. (Transgender it things make death unclean – contaminated).

And no, you cannot blame death for truly not wanting them because they contaminate not just earth but the spiritual realm as well.

No, death does not have a choice – death must accept them because the role of death is death and not life.

Death cannot give life hence death is death and not life. We know this but yet refuse to live a good life.

We all want to go up to see Good God but yet do nothing that is good and clean to get there.

We say we have the truth, which is your holy books, but each and every day we break the law and laws of Good God including the laws in our holy books.

As human beings we fail to realize that no books are holy. If that book isn't directly given to you by Good God then you cannot deem that book holy.

If Good God did not tell you directly to write a book or his book, then you cannot write one and say it is divinely inspired because no book is divinely inspired. Good God tells you and show you what he wants you to write and you cannot write lies – books of lies and deceit like the so called Jews. They say they are of God but are not of Good God because they write lies to deceive nations hence revelations told you about them. You cannot say you are God's chosen and lie like that come on now.

You are not God's chosen you are death's chosen as well as sins chosen because you write books of lies for sin and death to bring humanity to hell and burn.

No child of Good God can say they are of him and live in lies and for lies. Come on now. Like I've said Good God does not tell lies on us so why are we telling lies on him? Trust me many of these so called Jews will see hell because all that wrote lies about Good God and tell lies on Good God will have more than hell to pay in hell when it comes to death. None will see Good God. They will see death because their names as well as their children's names and yes the names of their families are written in hell – the book of the dead. Absolutely nothing they can do, can or will get their names out of death's book. No, not even the cutting of your hair, this I know now. As simple as death is loyal to death, he is loyal to Good God even more hence Death is our Judge, Jury and Executioner. This I know now hence I am telling you this.

Know that the messages Good God gives to you is also written and it is you that must relay the message back to humanity exactly as shown to you.

Good God does speak like I've said but rarely.

Dreams are also an important tool that he uses to show you things to come as well as happen in your life and the life of others. Trust me dreams are extremely important hence we have them.

Music is also important because he does lead you to the right music that you need to hear to strengthen you on the days you are weak.

As humans we know we are not to kill but yet each and every day we kill. Governments send our children to fight wars – battles that do not concern them.

We say we are going to have a new world order but yet the time of sin and death – evil is up by the end of 2013.

Evil lost its bid to fight and wage war on humanity because in all sin did, he did to kill and destroy, send humanity to hell to burn and die.

Like I've said, we know this but yet we believe – say lies are true.

Lies cannot be true when lies are death. Your ticket into hell where you will be enslaved burned and eventually die.

You have to protect your life and if you have not chosen Good God then your life is not protected.

If you say you've chosen Jesus – Christos then you are not protected. You will die because you accepted a false prophet that did not exist.

Good God does not deal in death and I've told you this. Nor would he commission anyone to die for wicked and sinful people.

It is not right nor is it fair for someone to die for your wrongs. Your wrongs are your wrongs and I've told you this.

There are no scapegoats with Good God only truth and if you have not truth then you cannot have everlasting life period.

Good God is not about dominion evil is.
Good God is not about death sin is.
Death is.
You the individual is.

Life is not about the flesh it's about the spirit – the energy or life within you. Hence I've told you the life you live in the living (physical) determines where you go in the grave or spiritual realm.

If you live an unclean life on earth (the physical) you cannot live a clean life in the grave (the spiritual).

If you knowingly or willingly kill in the physical (on earth) you cannot move forward in the spirit. You must move down to hell because you knowingly and willingly took a life – flesh. Hence the flesh is a part of the spirit. They are bound until the time that was allotted to the flesh is over.

These things I've told you. I've even told you about religion hence Good God has nothing to do with religion.

Religion was given to you by sin to bring you to your deaths and sin has and have succeeded in doing so because daily we use religion to kill and destroy the lives of others.

Religion is dirty and stink hence Good God is not a part of the devil's master plan of deceit. Goodness is what evil seek to destroy and each and every day evil succeeds because of us as humans.

We give power to wicked and evil people that have and has their own agenda and that is the agenda of sin and death.

The more we sin is the more we die.
The more we sin is the more it takes away from the goodness of the land.
The more we sin is the more earth dies.
The more we sin is the more our children die.
The more we sin is the more our future dies, meaning taken away from us.

All these things we know but refuse to do better for ourselves.

We were given false hope long ago and false hope cannot get you into Good God's kingdom, it can only get you into hell.

No one can buy time for you because time cannot be bought. *The reality is, if you constantly sin, do wrong, you are going to go to hell and die period. You cannot change this because it is the law and the law cannot change to please you or me.*

Like I said, we are the ones to let others tell us crap and sacrifice us to death. Hell is not pretty I've told you this.

I've told you what the fire looks like that is going to burn the spirit.

I've told you what death looks like in the different stages.

I've told you what Good God look like.

I've told you what his children look like.

I've told you what Satan look like.

It's up to you now to change you because no one on the face of this planet have or has the right religion. I am not the one to change you. You are the one to change you because I can't change you. No one can. Not even Good God. He gives us the right tools we need to survive, we are the ones to destroy them and listen to others say their way is right when we know that their way in not right but wrong.

If you say you are Muslim and you have the right religion then you are one of the spiritually dead. ***Islam or being Muslim has nothing to do with Good God it has all to do with spiritual death.*** I've told you Islam is a spiritual prison. If you want your spirit or soul to stay in the prison (s) of hell for infinite generations while burning harsher than hell itself then continue to join the Islamic nation. BUT KNOW THIS. *YOU WILL INFINITELY NEVER EVER SEE THE REALM OR ABODE OF GOOD GOD. NOR WILL YOUR CHILDREN SEE GOOD GOD'S REALM OR ABODE.*

No murderer or liar can enter Good God's abode hence you will infinitely and indefinitely never ever find a Muslim in Good God's Kingdom. ***TO BE A MUSLIM MEANS TO GO AGAINST LIFE – GOOD LIFE. HENCE THE KILLING THAT THESE PEOPLE DO BRINGS THEM AND YOU STRAIGHT TO HELL.***

*Allah means the Breath of Life yes but these people do not have the Breath of Life. Hence they go against life with the murders – killings that they do. **A Babylonian can never have life, he can only have death because death is what they believe in as well as participate in.***

To be a Muslim means you've joined the realm of the spiritual dead. This realm is the realm that fights against Good God and his children – good people. Hence no Muslim will or could possesses the Breath of Life which is Allelujah.

They (Muslims) willingly and knowingly kill then lie and say Allah – the Breath of Life is with them when they know that death – the God of war – Aries is with them.

All life is sacred but when it comes to humans – humanity, life is not sacred because we design to destroy and kill. And we do kill without remorse.

Hence many cannot answer for the crimes they do in the grave. We cannot kill and think it's okay because no one can create life by themselves. If they could there would be more universes and stars all around.

*The breath and power of life belongs not to man but to Good God and no one can possess this life or power if Good God has not given it to you. Hence I've told you **NO BABLYLONIAN IS IN GOOD GOD'S KINGDOM NOR ARE THEY ON HIS MOUNTAIN.***

Life is not a joke nor is God – Good God a joke. We should not take God – Good God for granted but yet each and every day we do this. Take him for granted and spit in his face with the lies we accept.

Tell me something. ***Did you not born with life? So how can God – Good God take life?***

Did it not say the wages of sin is death and truth is everlasting life? So why sin if you know that you are going to die?

Why not tell the truth and live?

Drinking blood and bathing in blood is not going to get you in Good God's abode. It's getting you in hell and you are going to burn and die. There are no ands ifs or buts about this because you chose blood and death over Good God. And you are truly nasty. It's a nasty and filthy demon that bathes in blood and drink blood and not even the demons of hell I've seen drinking blood. Nor do I want to see this gross nastiness either.

Sacrificing your children and others unto death by killing them is not going to get you in Good God's abode it's getting you in hell. Well you are going to go straight to hell. There are no ands ifs or buts about this because you willingly and knowingly took an innocent life. Wow. Trust me hell is smiling at you because you knowingly and willingly went against the **LAW OF LIFE THAT STATES THOU SHALT NOT KILL.**

But but but.

There are no buts. You did willingly sin and willful sins are infinitely and indefinitely not forgiven and I've told you this. You willingly went

against the law of life which is the law of God –
Good God.

You knew wrong from right and you willingly did
wrong, hence Good God cannot forgive you.
Meaning when your goodness can wipe out or
cancel out many of your wrongs, no, that is not
right because the goodness that you do truthful
and true can cancel out or wipe out many of
your sins but your goodness cannot wipe out or
cancel out willful sins because they were
willfully done. You knew there are no forgiveness
for them hence you do them anyway.

Yes it's October 23, 2013 and the end of man –
the devil's system of things in near hence to all
that is good and clean including Good God I
dedicate A Better Way by Jah Cure to all.

We need a better way hence I dedicate this song
to me as well because I truly need a better way.
And as I choose Good God all the way, I know I
am with him – saved.

Hence Russia and Vladmir Putin I truly do not
care if you do not listen to me. The young one (in
the dream she was your daughter) that is
pushing you to do all that is wrong will be your
own doing. At the end of the day, if you do not
wisen up and listen to the word of Good God
Russia will go down in flames like the United

States and there are no and if or buts about this. I don't give a damn about your politics because Good God don't care about it. **_Good God however truly cares about the people of Russia and it's not right for you to dick around with their lives like that._** At the end of the day, I delivered the message of God – Good God hence I've done my job. I did not fail him you will be the one to fail your country and people.

America did not listen to Marcus Mosiah Garvey and look at their hell hole of a national debt. Look at the disarray of the country. They failed Good God because the one that came to them and gave them the message of Good God was not white but black. I am no different hence if you do not take heed then good luck to Russia and your people because your land will be left barren and powerless. You now have the truth hence it's up to you to change the dirty sheets that are on your bed and prepare your people for the harvest that is to come. Russia is no exception to the harvest. Your people are going to die if you do not listen and what say you to Good God and your people. Many lands are going to become barren – void of food and water so truly think because what you are doing is wrong because your bed sheets are not exactly clean. Your wife is the clean one from the dream and you are the unclean one so truly clean yourself up and live. Like I said before, I will not draw the correlation to Gog and Magog because I know the difference. I know the strength and power of the bear hence I refuse the correlation of the two ancient cities that can be compared to Sodom and Gomorrah. No one can get me to draw this correlation because like I've said Gog and Magog did not exist.

No one wants to hear the truth but the truth cannot lie or kill. So truly look into things because Good God is trying to save your land and people and I don't know why. Like I said, you're all racist but still with your racist attitude Good God is trying to save your land and I so don't know why. Listen, in the case of Russia, I am not the one to question God – Good God and I will not do so because he knows best. You cannot treat your people unfair and unjust and say you are just. Nor can you say you are of Good God because you are not. Good God is fair and just hence no man can be like him when it comes to truth and justice. Yes I question his ethics but like I said I can do so because we have a true relationship and I am not fake nor do I hide my true feelings from him.

Having a good country and a stable economy does not mean you are to treat your people unfair or unjust. Bullying does not work because at the end of the day if Good God say you must be removed from office there is not a damned thing you can do about it. You will be removed by any means necessary including death. And no, Good God does not kill anyone it means your sins will catch up to you and if your sins outweigh your goodness death can automatically take you because your name is in deaths book.

Trust me when Good God finds the right person that is honest and true to the people of Russia no prison cell, no attempts on their lives, no lies, no injustice will work because that person was chosen by Good God to replace you and you will be replaced. Bullies does not stay forever in office because truth is what Good God seeks and from he has the truth in that one person nothing you do can or will stop them because Good God will chose and bless them over you.

Like I said, I don't care if you don't like me. I am not here to win a popularity contest. I've done my job by delivering the message of God – Good God and I so have to leave it there. As for you Prokhorov I cannot say anymore because I dreamt about you this morning but can't remember the dream so I am going to leave you alone for now. The dream was not negative hence I am so going to leave you alone today. So later King Kong. You're tall hence you are King Kong in my book. And I am not insulting you because you know the true long King Kong had for her. Watch the movie and you will know what I am talking about.

Yes people the dreams are coming again. This morning I dreamt I was on my balcony and I looked up in the night sky and I saw planes coming and going. There was a helicopter and a commercial airline (plane). They were on the same path. The commercial plane flew above the helicopter and the propellers of the helicopter caught the commercial airline or jet and got stuck. I thought the plane was going to crash down and explode but it did not crash. Apparently Jay Z and Beyonce were on the helicopter because Jay Z stared the helicopter to safety. I could see the inside of the helicopter and it had cars lined up and it was the cars he was staring or shuffling for the plane and helicopter not to crash. He landed safely and Beyonce came to my door and I closed it shut – locked the door so that she could not come into my house. My telephone was left outside the door and she took it to call someone but I opened the door and grabbed it from her so that she could not use it. She smiled – had a smile on her face and I called the police to say that Beyonce was at my home, but I knew that they would not believe me and the man or officer on the other end of the line did not believe me. She had her mark but her mark was white. Her mark looked like the flag of Quebec. Oh man how do I describe it? The arch on the left and right of the flag of Quebec was what her mark looked like except the direction was curved.

The curve above is the direction of the mark. This is the best picture I can find. You can use a bow and arrow but a bow and arrow is not the best picture.

Suffice it to say she did not succeed with me and she left but before she left she had a bunch of globe grapes in her hand and she started to eat it – meaning she ate one. After leaving she wrote this in the sky. The sky was blue with white clouds. THE MESSAGE SHE WROTE IN THE SKY WAS *"I AM WHAT I AM."*

Hence I know now the meaning of the I Am.

<u>Good God is not the I AM, EVIL IS. EVIL IS THE I AM hence evil cannot change.</u> They are the way they are because they accepted evil and was born of evil. Evil is in their blood hence they were born of the bloodline of evil. I know I've confused you but I can't explain my statement properly for you to overstand and or comprehend.

JUST KNOW THAT GOOD GOD IS NOT THE I AM, EVIL IS.

ONWARDS I GO WITH THE DREAM.

After reading the message I left with my son and we were walking on this dirt road with green grass on both sides of us. I call it green grass but it could be young sugar cane growing because the green grass or sugar cane was tall and abundant. Trust me the road was long and Jay Z came after me but this man – black man that seemed to be an officer caught up to him and was questioning him. He was trying to get Jay Z to confirm that he was a part of the Illuminati but Jay Z did not confess. He evaded the questions. He gave the right answers but it was not the full confirmation or confession the man needed. My son and I walked ahead. I don't know how I came up to this place – office that sold homes. I don't know what took place but this white man in a black suit and dark hair. He was about five four or five six and just right in build. Not too fat or skinny but just right and good looking. I guess he got impatient and sold the property to someone else and I think he said if you snooze you lose. But he beat Jay Z at his game. That was that dream and trust me I could not go back to sleep because I wanted to keep the message. I was lazy to get up and write the message people.

Man oh man the people of the world is so gone.

I also dreamt Joe Jonas making the sign for the head of Horus.

Wow, the people of the world is gone and we can thank the devil and man for this. **Well man because the book of sin did say Satan was going to make the world bow down to him and he's done that easily because the world meaning humanity follow the book of sin to a T as well as to their graves.** (The so called holy bible that was commissioned by King James is called the book of sin and he King James was Illuminati). Free Mason for those who do not know. Today nothing has changed because he Satan got power and now he has given Jay Z power. And yes I know the power that Jay Z got.

Wow because many do not know that what Satan, no Melchesidec has given them on earth, he cannot give them in death. Hence hell and their place in the pit (s) of hell with death. And yes many of you will not comprehend the Satan giving Jay Z power.

Listen people if you think in millions you will be lost. You have to think in billion not trillions. Trillions are what's exchanged on the stock market – what is traded in business. If you **are**

not a billionaire you are not at the top of the food chain hence THE NEW WORLD ORDER OF SIN THAT SATAN'S FINANCIAL BACKERS WANT TO IMPLEMENT.

The new world order of sin will infinitely and indefinitely not happen because the time of sin and death is over and Good God did find his one that he is looking for to save the world. Do not look at me because like I've told you, I am not her. I was told the one to save humanity "she must live clean." Like I've said, don't look at me because I too have sinned and have sin on my plate. My record book has sin in it. All I am here to do is deliver the messages given to me nothing else.

Like I said, I cannot comprehend why anyone would want to go to hell and burn. People tell you there is no hell and you believe it. Hell is real hence Melchesidec or Satan as you call him had 24000 years to deceive and that time is up at the end of 2013. Satan can no longer rule.

1313 2032 and 2132 are the three dates I got.

I've told you humanity lost 2132 hence the destruction or death of evil's system of things is before 2032. Evil can no longer kill to sustain and maintain sin and death.

All that evil did to deceive and kill must return unto them hence the harvest come for the wicked globally.

I've told you lands are going to break away as well as become barren. No food or water will be allotted the wicked and evil hence Cannibalism will become the norm in many societies in this day and time.

You gave your life over to death hence death must take you – feed you and I know that death cannot feed you anything apart from give you a harsh and painful life and death. This will be the reality of humanity real soon because we made it so.

We accepted the offerings of the devil which is death hence death must now take his people on a mass scale.

I've told you it was the Egyptians, Persians and Phoenicians that took us out of the Garden of Eden – Zion. So if these are the people that took us out of Zion why are we associating with them?

Why are we doing business with them?

Why are we fighting alongside them and for them?

Why are we marrying them?

Why are we eating and drinking with them?

Why are we going into their lands?

Why are we polluting our lands by having them in it? When we have them in our lands are we not disrespecting God – Good God?

Are we not saying to Good God Fuck You? I can do as I please and have who I please in my land – the land you have given me but can't produce a GLC (God Land Certificate) for.

Like I've said, nothing changes in death because we are the ones to disobey the law and laws of Good God by following people that have not your best interest at heart. And once again to the members of Scientology you have a bye, meaning a pass. Good God have and has given you a bye, a pass to walk away from that fraudulent system. ***No one can buy you a place in life for a billion years because no one can buy life.*** You are to live life good and clean. Take your bye or pass and tell Good God thanks and live your life good and clean.

All Good God requires are honest, good, true and clean people. If you are living clean then you are good to go.

So because someone robbed you of your right, Good God is giving you a chance to come clean and live clean. ***No one has the right to hold you hostage and tell you that you should live this way or that way when they of themselves are not of Good God.*** I don't even know what they are of because in truth not even the devil wants them.

Yes you have evil organizations out there hence everything is based on monetary gain and manipulating you. Once you have been manipulated and conditioned then you have no say. You have not worth to yourself. You've become their worth or commodity to be traded at will because you are their money making machine.

Like I've said, if you are living good and clean along with your children – family, then you have nothing to worry about. You will go up to see Good God. But if you are living unclean then you will go do to hell to die. But before you die your spirit must burn in hell for a period of time. Like I've told, you there is no water in hell and on earth it is not the flesh that feels pain but the spirit. If we cannot handle the pain and pains of earth there is no way we are going to handle it in hell.

The pain is more severe so do not strive to go there. Meaning do not strive to go to hell. Yes we make mistakes but life is not about harping on our mistakes. Learn from your mistakes and grow. Life is about good growth – goodness and if we cannot live good on earth we cannot live good in hell.

Do not strive to have the mark of the beast. Strive to have the mark and breath of life so that you can live with Good God.

Good God is not about pain and no matter I argue with him, you cannot do what I do because you do not know Good God like I do.

Yes I can hold him accountable because he knew the pain associated with hell and he should have done a better job in protecting his people. I know he Good God cannot force us to accept him or do the things that is right but hell should be your motivation not to go there meaning go to hell.

Hell is not pretty and the more we sin is the further we go in hell.

Our sins are our sins and I've told you this hence many things I say F them because they are not me.

I am not here to blame hence I say F slavery because I know my own people sold their own into slavery. Hence I do not blame the white man alone, I blame the black man also.

A man cannot come into your land and wage war unless you invite him in. Go back to your book of sin. Satan was not in the garden of Good God contrary to what your book of sin or bible say.

Eve was the one to let him into her garden and he did deceive her. He told her what she wanted to hear despite Good God telling her not to listen. SHE LET SIN IN hence the black race are the way we are until this day. We continually let sin into our world and when sin destroy us we complain and say sin isn't fair. Why let sin into your life then? You know sin brings hardships and pain so why sin? You too have to blame yourself because you did wrong and you know right from wrong.

WE PAY THE PRICE WHEN WE SIN. I KNOW THIS BECAUSE I AM PAYING THE PRICE AND THE PRICE IS NOT PRETTY. This price is stress and all the ills that are associated with stress.

Aries can't just get up and wage war against you if you have done him nothing. Nor can

death come and take you if you have not sinned. And don't bring the death of a baby into this because death can take your child or children if you have sinned. Meaning given yourself over to death. Once you have given yourself over to sin and death then your children automatically becomes death's children.

But but but

No buts. This is the law of death. What is given unto death he keeps – takes because you gave it to him.

Our sins are death hence when we sin we give ourselves over to death. We are telling death we want him to take us to hell and burn and this is what happens today. More so today than that of the past.

We invite evil in and when evil wreak havoc in our country we say they are unfair.

Don't even think it because despite what you say the United States was invited into your country to kill. Yes they do wrong because your fight is not the US's fight hence they will go down to hell and rightfully so.

Babylon wants control of the global market but like I said, God – Good God would never give them the power to control and rule humanity again. They had 24000 years hence your four and twenty elders.

Yes it is said and I've said man cannot live more than 120 years but I say on this day I mislead you and that statement is a lie. ***Evil cannot live beyond a thousand years. The life span of evil is one thousand years but good hath no life span. The life of good is forever ever. Hence good cannot die but evil dies hence humanity dies.***

Like I said, we readily accept lies and refuse the truth and when things do not work out for us we run to God and say why me and forgive me. But Good God cannot forgive sins made against our fellow man. The person you wronged are the ones to forgive you. God – Good God can only forgive sins against him. I've told you this hence I told you if you cannot forgive a man in the living you cannot forgive him in death.

You can but I can't. I have to forgive him in the living. He must ask for forgiveness in the living not in death.

Evil knows his end but ***Good*** hath no end. The death of flesh is not the end of life. Your spirit is your true life hence you are to live life good and true – clean

And like I've said, the reason why you don't hear the dead cry like a bitch in the grave is because there are too much noise around us. If there were no noise you would hear them and hold your ears to the amount of crying you would hear.

Hence I tell you to stop buying into the bullshit of the churches as well as wicked and evil people. At the end of the day your soul and or spirit matters. It is vital to you.

Do live to go down to hell but live to go up to Good God.

I don't give a shit if you don't like me as long as God – Good God truly loves me because at the end of the day you now have the truth. You cannot say Good God never gave you to truth so that you can overcome the harvest that is to come.

Yes the New World Order is almost here but this order is not for the wicked but for the good and pure at heart.

Evil will lose it all because the death – the three deaths were tossed into the fire hence death died. Death's people must die with him also. Death cannot be resurrected and rightfully so because like I said, goodness cannot die only evil can and will die.

As humans we say we want life but do all to destroy and kill life. So tell me now, how do you want life if you kill it each and every day?

Yes this is Blackman Redemption the Truth and it feels good today because I know better must come and all evil will and must die.

The Babylonian System must die hence Babylon must go down. Their kingdom is falling and no matter what humanity do to give evil power, they must fail because evil is only for a time and then all must pay. The evils that humanity do must be returned to sender.

Hence Good God I am coming to you because it seems you don't get me. Like I've told you, sin and evil did not create this universe, you did and you can no longer give sin and evil a home because you are hurting your people and you as God and Good God cannot blame them (your people) or any of them if they say they hate you and you were not there for them.

Like I've told you, I am fed up and ready to walk but because of truth, I cannot leave you because

I did give you my word of truth and right now you are making me regret my decision.

Like I've said, loving us so is not loving us true. You cannot say you love us so and then turn around and let your people suffer at the hands of wicked and evil people.

How much more sacrifices should death have before you intervene and say enough is enough? Right now evil has control of the land – earth and instead of saying this cannot be you continue to let the spell stay.

The spell that was cast on man – humanity must be broken and you refuse to do it.

Like I've said and told you, those that did not choose you, leave them the hell alone. Do not provide for them because they did not choose you. The ones that truly love you and have kept true to you provide them with your true and good land so that when the harvest fully comes they will have enough food to eat and water to drink. You are the one that we trust with our lives hence you must help us to sustain and maintain ourselves in the harvest that is coming. You have to start separating us from evil in goodness and in truth.

You cannot say you are Good God and make your children – people suffer. ***When you do this it would me you did not truly love your people. We do not need false hope we need your truth and true love.***

You cannot let us continue to suffer. It is not fair nor is it just. Just as you are hurting we are hurting too. Remember we did not ask for this we were born into it. Death is all we know because death is what's being taught to us and it is not right.

We need good life and if you are not giving us good life we will continue to follow death to our graves.

Good God, despite the time line of sin and death your children should not be witnesses to sins and I've told you this. What sin does to deceive his people your children should not have to witness it.

What sins children do to pay allegiance to sin and death your children should not see nor witness because sin's children hath nothing to do with good life. They have all to do with death hence they feast off blood and pray to death. They also pay death to kill them hence the exchange of money it death's whore houses – churches.

When we see the sins of sin and how prettied up sin looks we follow sin. This is exactly what we did and look at us now. Wallowing in our messes and can't get out.

You allocated sin time and look at the damage sin has done. You have the ability to change this hence I ask you to lift the spell and spells of sin and death and let humanity choose for self. We cannot just see death alone; we also need to see life – good life. ***Sin cannot pretty up everything when we know sin is not pretty but ugly.***

You are hurting yes but you are not the only one hurting in all of this. I see the evils of humanity and how evil has full enjoyment of the earth and you let them. How about your people? Hence I say you do not make me happy because you see the ills of the earth and turn a blind eye to it. Yes this is my view and you have to do better.

Sin is doing his job what about you?

Why the hell should it be easy for evil and hard for good?

If you as Good God truly cared for the safety and sanity of your good and true people, you would provide for them a good and true home. But because you care not we are living amongst the wicked and stressing.

So you cannot say you are not at fault in any of this because you are.

Good Life isn't about hurt and pain nor is it about strife and war. It's about good. It's about happiness and when you fail to give your people happiness then you have failed us royally. And yes we will turn to sin and acknowledge sin over you because it seems like this is what you want. You want your children to fail.

Yes I can say you failed us because in my eyes to a certain degree you have. Tell me something Good God. Who the hell wants to live in a nasty home or planet? I am striving to get to you but how can I get to you when all around me is unclean?

How can I strive to be with you when evil surrounds me?

You have the ability to return evil to sender and I've told you this but you are the one not to exercise your authority.

You cannot let evil bind and trample down your people anymore because at the end of the day you are wrong in doing so.

Like I said, no one want to feel pain and if we are left in pain will we not do painful things?

If we are left in sin will we not do sinful things?

Now tell me, how do you justify yourself in all of this?

Like I said, filth is something that I do not like hence I truly love clean. But I do not live in cleanliness because of my children and I am ready to flee.

I know the clean road but it you do not aide us when it comes to cleanliness how can we be fully clean in you? And please do not use the evils of this world to justify you because you cannot with me.

Remember no child asked to be evil and many of us live what we learn meaning live what our parents taught us. Hence if our parents were taught wrong there is no way they can teach us right and you know this. ***As a parent you have to teach right and if you Good God do not teach right we will do wrong and this is what we have done.***

You allowed false teachings to take precedence over your truth now look at

humanity. Fighting for this and that religion thinking they are going to find you.

You allowed evil to make us lost so nothing you say or do in my book can justify you. Right is right and I refuse to give you right when you know you are wrong.

If evil continually tell us lies and that he is god will we not believe him over you?

Is this not what evil has and have done over the centuries and now that we are down to the last hour you are acting and thinking it is going to be easy?

People are set in their ways already and like I said, I refuse to tell anyone to come to you or choose you.

You are Good God and you should not have to plea with man – humanity to accept the truth or you. We all know right from wrong but instead of doing right we do wrong and expect someone to die for our wrongs – sins.

This I blame on you Good God because you could have stopped this lie but you allowed people that know nothing of your goodness tell lies on you when they wrote the book of sin. These people say they are Jews – your people but yet they are the devil's own because they lay claim to the lies and books of the Babylonians. If they were your people they would know about the Ethiopians and how they the Ethiopians sold you out as well as sold their own people out hence Israel is no more.

They write books of lies for sin but yet they say they are your people. Now tell me this. Can your people – true people tell lies on you?

Can your true people write books of lies about you?

Who amongst your true people can stand up and say Jesus was your son, when we know you have no sons' only daughters. Hence evil did all it can to have daughters like you to say he is you.

You know evil is the slave master of humanity but you fail to let humanity know this.

Life on earth did not have to be this way regardless of the time limit or line you gave to the four and twenty elders. Sin had no place with man and you know this but all changed and look at us today. Everyone saying they have you when they have not you.

Everyone saying they are going to go to heaven or paradise when you know their heaven or paradise is hell.

Yes there is many more hence sin has his book deceiving humanity. Sin have humanity bowing down to death in his whore houses - churches. All that Satan said he would do he has done and he can thank humanity for this. He can thank humanity for giving him the victory over you.

Tell me something Good God, how can you truly justify yourself when you know the death of humanity – the death of flesh and spirit?

None of us can justify sin because life isn't about death it's about life – the goodness of life and you know this. So how can you love us so when I truly cannot find any truth in you on this day. Meaning truth in you loving us so.

We all want a better life and if we cannot have a better life on earth how can we have it in the grave?

No we cannot take our earthly possessions with us. We can however take our goodness with us, because our goodness is our truths hence everlasting life and you know this.

We all want a better way of life Good God but we cannot have this riddled with sin and living amongst sin and in sin.

You know the truth because you are the truth but yet you've failed humanity when it comes to the truth.

It is not good to love because love hurts and you know this. Hence I advocate truth and true love because true love cannot hurt. True love cannot lie and you know this so why can't you love true?

Why can't you do things in truth?

Yes I know you do this but I still have to question you and remind you of all these things.

Like I said, true love is what I advocate and it will be that way until my spirit gets or come to you. I will not give up on truth and neither should you.

Like I said, evil had his 24000 years. A thousand years each for his elders – princes of darkness and that time is almost up. Now the preparation begins for the harvest and I will feel sorry for no evil one or person.

I will not beg you for evil and wicked people because they know what they have done. They also know what they were doing. I will beg you for the ones I truly love including beg you for the people who have done good unto me and I've done this in The New Book of Life – Judgement. I will not change this book because these are my truths and goodness onto you as well as to the people that have and has done good unto me.

Good God I know good life hence I thank you for being you. You know when I write in this way I need you to truly think and see the inequality of sin. Sin had no right to cause so much death and destruction on earth and you know this. Like I said you, are our right and no one should come and take you from us. ***I refuse to take evil from evil so why is evil taking you from us?***

I did not choose evil, I chose the goodness of life. I chose true and everlasting and forever ever good life that which is you. So why is evil trying all it can for me to fail you?

What right does evil have to do this?

Nothing that you say Good God can justify this. Hence I say you are not right because you continuously allow us to live amongst sin. Why should I have to be subject to seeing the crap that sin do and does?

What should I have to be subject to the shit that sin promotes on television, radio and internet?

Why should I have to see sin's puppets of nastiness that have been medically enhanced to look pretty when they are not? They are disgusting and ugly – sinful.

I need my way to be clear and sin is not pretty so why are you Good God allowing this? When you let us continue to see this crap are you not telling us it's okay to do sinful things?

Are you not condoning sin as well?

Are you as Good God not saying it's okay to live in sin and amongst sin?

Are you not saying it's okay to be sinful?

Yes I know otherwise but today the otherwise does not fly. You cannot justify keeping your people in nastiness. All you are doing as Good God is keeping us away from you and bringing us closer to hell if not into hell. And in so doing, you are infinitely and indefinitely wrong – sinful.

You cannot continue to let your people live in sin. When you continue to do this it means you are not truthful but sinful.

No, I am not you but you have a responsibility to your people and that responsibility is to keep us away from sin and evil infinitely and indefinitely.

You need to be truthful to us because if you are not truthful to us we cannot be truthful to you and you infinitely know this.

Hence if we know not the truth how can we be truthful?

Yes I'm searching for a better way (Jah Cure). Hence I say and will forever say, I don't give a damn if you don't like as long as you Good God truly loves me.

So to all that think I want your soul, I do not want or need your soul. You need it hence I will never ever, infinitely never ever convert anyone to Good God. You cannot convert anyone to good life, you must and have to live it – live a good and clean life.

Good God never told anyone to convert anyone to him because good life is given. We are the ones to destroy and kill it.

Your spirit and or soul is important to you hence you are not to desecrate the body. When you desecrate the body, you are desecrating Good God. Yes the Female God. We are the iron of the earth hence I've shown you the breakdown of Female in another book.

Yes I am rough and tough but sometimes you have to be this way for humanity to learn and comprehend.

Listen to me. No one can sell you God – Good God because God and or Good God cannot be bought and sold but we sure as hell can buy death and do buy death. Hence we do things in the reverse.

Trust me no one can tell me that Good God say speak for him because he Good God have a voice of his own and he does use it.

What he need you to teach he will show you on a school wall. Schools represent education – to teach.

Anything written in the sky, blue and white sky at nights represents death – failure as well as evil. Hence as it is in heaven so it is on earth. I could be wrong on this but until I see otherwise and is told otherwise it will stay evil. I will let you know if this changes.

Walking with Good God is a learning process and as you grow you get and see the truth. Hence I worry not about what humanity will say about me. I don't care if they call me the anti - Christ or the devil. Been there done that hence the words in these books are good's weapon against all facet of evil.

Like I've said, I don't want or need your soul and or spirit because mine is secure with Good God. If it was not he would not have asked me to write him a book twice and like I've said, I've written many.

No, I do not have a bucket list nor do I need one. At times I see the beauty of different countries before my eyes when I sleep, hence the spirit travels when the flesh is at rest.

Yes it's October 25, 2013 and the dreams are coming again but this time they are so strange. Man this dream is so weird hence I can't make heads or tails of it. I am confused because I know something bad is going to happen to Jamaica but yet I am being kept from seeing the destruction of the land. Wow it's weird because like I've said time and time again, I will not cry for the people of Jamaica because I truly know the wickedness of some of them. They failed Good God hence Judah went a whoring like the whoring Judas's that are called the Israelites. Yes the Ethiopians. The ones that stabbed Good God in his back by trampling him down in his holy place, hence the Ethiopians can lay claim to Babylonian lands including the land of Nod.

This is why I tell you, Good God cannot trust black people because in all that he has and have given us, we sell it, disrespect it, disrespect self and people including land and heritage – Good God.

This morning I had the weirdest dream involving Lava. I am not sure if the land is Jamaica but I think it is. I saw the land cracking; no not cracking because the earth was cracked. I saw the lava or fire in between the cracks. So I truly don't know. ***I cannot worry myself about the Jamaica because it seems as if death is teasing me. Showing me bits and pieces of what's to come.*** Yes this has been going on for years and I am truly tired of the bits and pieces because in truth I don't think anything can save Jamaica right now.

I know it's sad to say but it is my truth and reality because I do not believe in miracles. All that is ordained is set in time and it is humanity to reach that point in time and claim their blessings or damnation. Hence I tell you about physical and spiritual time. This is the second time I am seeing lava so if it's not Jamaica somewhere is going to get a lava bath. I did not see a volcano erupting and spewing hot rocks. Each time I see this dream, it's as if the lava was coming up from the ground. The earth itself is being eroded and lava coming up. It's funny because the night before I dreamt about the land close to where I grew up was eroded. You could see the pit or crater that was left from the land being eroded. It was not deep but you could see how and where the land eroded, now to see lava coming up from the ground. Wow.

Yes these dreams are weird but what can I do or say. This is the reality of the things I see. Certain things are hard to put together and I will not put them together.

All I can gather or say from this dream is. If the lava is coming up from the ground and the ground is being eroded, then I can safely say that Jamaica is going to be in for heavy drought. No, I won't speculate because like I said, I think its Jamaica. So everyone scrap my thoughts. I will leave well enough alone and see what unfolds in Jamaica.

Remember the island was deemed unclean by Good God so I guess the lava rising from the ground will be their forever ever punishment because they did sin vile and wicked in the eyes and sight of Good God. ***June 1692 was a testament where Port Royal sank. Maybe this time around it will be the entire island that will sink and then humanity can say Judah is no more.***

Yes the end of the year is winding down and there isn't much to do a part from watch and wait – see. Yes you can hate me and dislike me but it matters not to me because the harvest comes and many lands will be left barren – without food and water.

Like I said, we made it so because we did forget, ***"THE WAGES OF SIN IS DEATH."***

Things did not have to be this way but it's the choice we made. Like I said, we would rather live in lies and commit sin rather than hear the truth and live for and by the truth. Now the end is near and many will cry why me God?

Did I not do this, this and this?

Did I not praise and worship you? And many of you will hear you did not praise nor did you worship me. You worshipped death and a dead god. A false prophet and demon that did not exist; a false prophet that said he was my son; a false prophet that said he died for your sins, a false prophet that said you had to wash in blood and eat the flesh of the dead. All these things you believed in as well as participated in and all these things are not me.

As the God of life – truth, I cannot lie nor can I participate in death. Life is not death, it is life and I gave everyone and everything good life. You as humans just destroyed the goodness that I have given you. You accepted the devil's own and unto death you must go.

Know this, as the god of Truth, I cannot take life nor do I take life. Death takes your life depending on the life you live on earth. If you live good, truthful and clean, death cannot take you because you do not belong to death, you belong to me.

If you live an unclean and dirty life you belong to death because you are unclean and all that I do is clean. I cannot dirty myself because of man hence I will infinitely and indefinitely never send anyone to die for anyone including my own.

IF I AS GOD – GOOD GOD SENT SOMEONE TO DIE FOR YOU, INCLUDING DIE FOR YOUR SINS THEN I WOULD BE A MURDERER; A KILLER JUST LIKE DEATH. I WOULD BE

DEATH NOT LIFE. Hence many lies have been told on me and many of you believe these lies including participate in them.

None of you asked me for the truth by coming directly to me. You believe that someone must act on your behalf when it comes to me. Hence you believe Jesus is your interceder.

I am God why would I need an interceder when it comes to me and you?

Are you not capable of speaking for yourself?

Do you not have a voice to speak?

In all you do you believe and do not know.

Knowledge is what I give not belief hence there are no beliefs in my abode.

If you are not truthful, good and clean you cannot come into my good abode. Nor can you be my messenger.

If you are not truthful, good and clean you cannot live with me hence I am not the I am nor am I death.

I cannot be what I created, I must be me. I must be Good God – good and true because **_"TRUTH_**

IS EVERLASTING LIFE" and no matter how man alter the truth to suit their father which is sin, the truth must prevail.

Hell did not come about like that. Hell came about due to your sins.

You as human beings created hell with your sins hence your death is your own doing and no one else's. Your death is not my doing but yours.

You are the ones to want to die because if you did not want to die you would not sin.

Like I said, Good God never commissioned anyone to die for you. If he Good God did that then he would be a murderer. He Good God would be going against life and he cannot do that.

Look at it. His son died and all of humanity lived.

He died for the sins of man – humanity but yet humanity keeps on sinning until this day.

He died but yet sin lived. Would not sin have died with him if he died to save you from sin?

He sacrificed himself to and for the sins of man – humanity, but sin is still with man – humanity?

Now tell me what sense did his death make?

Did he not die in vain because humanity have and has sinned wickeder than our ancestors of old?

Know this, no one can tell lies on Good God and expect to live beyond the spiritual realm.

I've told you our flesh is just a conductor and or prison for the spirit. The flesh goes back home to Mother, Mother Earth. The spirit moves on to higher life or death depending on the life you live on earth.

Your spirit is the one to face judgement, life or death then. And if your spirit goes down meaning your eye in the triangle is turned down then there is no way you are going up to see Good God. You are going to die and there are no ands ifs or buts about this. This is your reality hence no one can die for your sins.

Like I've said, the good people that Good God gave to me I am responsible for. Hence I've asked Good God to share my goodness with them. My goodness must go towards saving them but I will not die for anyone nor will I condone slackness.

If you are not true to life and truthful and honest to life in a good and true way, then you cannot share in the goodness of Good God with me and his people – children. ***So if Good God say, Michelle I give you the decision to let humanity in, trust me many in humanity would never get in including some of my children.*** From I have your record of Good and Evil before me, trust me woe be unto many of you because ***absolutely no its things – transgender abomination of life and death would get in.*** None would because I wouldn't even put them in hell to contaminate death. I would create a harsher and hotter hell for them. Yes people I would put a smile on death's face brighter than that of the sun.

No German woo Nelly. Oh man if I could reserve the judgement for them trust me I would more than go beyond protocol because every hurt and hate that I have in my body would come out. Trust me Good God would shake his head and say and I thought death was fierce but no Michelle you are more fierce than death himself. Like I've said, nothing on the face of earth or in Good God's abode can get me to forgive them for what they did to the flag of life (The Jamaican Flag which is the flag of Good God). No even Good God can wane my more than infinite spiritual anger that I have for them.

If I had the chance wow, no German would see or live with Good God except for the Jamaican

Germans because they fall under the banner of Good God. Yes they can cuss me but trust me my anger is true and real, hence I truly leave Germany to Good God. I leave them in his hands and care because he truly knows how I feel about them. Hence he asked me to write him a book again after my venting.

No one knows about life and the goodness of life but yet we pass our place like we are anyone.

We stink and cannot clean ourselves but yet we pass our place. Some people don't even bathe for a week. Some only bathe once per year and Good God is to find favour in us when we run from water – cleanliness. Please!!!!!!!!!!!

Yes the dreams are coming but yet I can't do anything about them.

Some I can't remember but I know I had them. These are the ones I am not to remember.

Man yesterday was a day because someone was in my house but I cannot tell what they looked like. Sometimes I hate ghost. I guess the noise they make is their way of saying they are in your home and not to fear them.

Sometimes I wish I could see them face to face and talk to them like I would talk to another human being. And no I do not envy those that can see them face to face. I see them in my dreams yes.

When I close my eyes I can see them yes but to actually talk to one face to face would be so cool. No because to me the dead should stay dead but for some reason they find me when they have something to say. I know when they are around because some are in black clothing and some in white clothing. Sometimes it's just a black shadow you see behind you. I hate when the shadows come close. I know why the shadows come close. Let's just say when I am rude to Good God in a certain way the shadows come. They don't come for any other reason but my rudeness and I have to stop being rude a certain way. So Good God truly forgive me for my rudeness but you know my frustrations, pains and sorrows.

YES THE HARVEST COMES AND MANY LANDS WILL BE LEFT BARREN.

The lava comes up now from the earth hence man will plant food and yield nothing.

Man will seek water to drink and there will be no water to drink.

Man will be looking for food and will find none.

Man will seek the resources of the land and will find none.

Woe be unto man because they sinned reckless in the eyes and sight of Good God.

And to the Rasta's, not because you are Rasta's mean that you are going to see Good God. Trust me you won't because you **_TELL HUMANITY BABYLON IS A FRAUD AND THEIR SYSTEM IS WICKED BUT YET YOU WORSHIP A BABYLONIAN._**

YOU CLAIM SELASSIE IS YOUR GOD WITHOUT KNOWING THAT HIS HISTORY IS THAT OF A BABYLONIAN.

YOU CLAIM ALL IN THE NAME OF GOD BUT YET YOU LIVE LIKE THE HEATHENS AND DO WHAT THE HEATHENS DO.

YOU CLAIM ALL IN THE NAME OF GOD BUT YET READ FROM THE BOOKS OF BABYLON AS WELL AS TEACH YOUR CHILDREN FROM THESE BOOKS – THE BOOKS OF BABYLON.

Yes all this you do hence the lots of you are going to go down in the flames of hell.

Lox yes Lox where do I begin because your lox is the hair of the dead. ***Hence lox – the locking of your soul in hell.***

You know not the state of your hair hence you walk in death and talk in death – know not the unity of the lox in death.

For those who know you can have a lox but the lox is not for all hence God's true children cannot rock this look. ***It is truly forbidden for us to do so.*** You can twist your hair but you cannot lock it hence the crown of white gold, well silver atop your head. **Good God's true children must have their hair low cut at all times.** Meaning the ones he chose to deliver his message cannot have long hair, it must be low cut. All others can have long hair but Good God's chosen cannot have long hair. It is forbidden.

This may be contradiction to some but the true truth to all.

It's October 27, 2013 early in the morning and I have to get this in. I've been having some weird dreams lately as I've told you and this is a weird one also. My dreams started out with wrestling and that too was weird hence I am listening to Fred Hammond's No Weapon. I need this song this morning because of this awkward dream that involved Lil Wayne. I don't know if he was doing a concert or a music video. He was performing and this wall was there. The wall was filled with graffiti. He went up to the wall and this light came upon him as if electrocuting him. The electrocuted it electrocuted him Zitchi (spelt exactly as seen) appeared in a rectangle shaped box. I don't know what Zitchi means nor do I know the language hence I am leaving this alone. If you can tell me what Zitchi means then by all means go ahead? Google has nothing on Zitchi but if you know the meaning of this word like I said, let me know because it does not seem as if this word is good.

No I can't go back to sleep because it seems like Good God wants me to talk about music and how these artists have perverted and destroyed his art – beauty.

And no like I said, Satan was not a beautiful singer that resided with Good God because nothing unclean can be in Good God's abode. So when the book of sin talks about crap like this I know otherwise.

If you are created **_GOOD_** you cannot turn because you are void of all sin. Nor can you sin. You are pure and of the true light of Good God and Satan was never good nor was he pure hence he could not have resided with Good God. Infinitely and indefinitely impossible.

Music is beautiful and it is we as humans that are destroying the beauty of it.

We as humans are the ones to bring negative forces into music hence killing the beauty of songs – truth.

Greed right now is the foundation for humanity and it is this greed that is going to destroy us all.

Like I've said, many of these artist – musicians have and has used friends, family and colleagues as sacrifices unto death. ***Many of you in society still buy their music and parade around like they have done nothing wrong.*** *Go back to Bob Marley's Babylon System. He told you that the Babylon System is a vampire because they graduate thieves and murderers. He told you of this long ago hence the sacrificing of animal and human life unto the dead will not stop.* Truly listen to this song and you will hear the truth because he is not wrong. *We are the ones to love lies and accept them and when these lies don't work out for us we run to Good God and complain.* Like I've said, it's over now because Good God is no one's bitch. We are to show him respect and don't even look at me and the way I write because this is me with Good God. I refuse to lie to him or be a hypocrite when it comes to him or anyone.

I more than infinitely truly love him and I've told you this hence he is my best friend and good All. My pain is his pain because I make him feel my pain as well as know it. He's been trying with us and we as humans are the ones to let him down and choose evil over him. Hence I tell him to leave death's children alone. ***Billions did not choose him hence he cannot provide for wicked and evil people anymore.*** He Good God is upholding slackness and nastiness as well as contributing to the growth of all facets of evil. Like I said, he cannot say he loves us so and continue to allow evil to destroy his land (s) and people. Evil did not create this earth and universe he Good God did. ***Evil got a free ride with Eve (Evening) and took it hence the time line of sin.***

In all that evil has and have done is to destroy all that Good God has and have given us to maintain the flesh and spirit.

Good God never gave us anything for evil to destroy. We allow evil to destroy it all because we believe death is life.

Yes this is what we are taught but yet again I say, not one of us went to Good God or God and say God or Good God, why do we have to die to find you?

Why should someone have to die to save us from sin?

Why should someone have to die for us to see you and talk to you?

Are sins not death? So how can someone die to save us from death when the flesh dies – must go back to its original source?

Why should we have to shed blood for our sins to be remitted?

We accepted blood hence the shedding of blood hath to do with a woman's menstrual cycle. Each month she shed's blood so how can the shedding of blood remit our sins?

Is blood not nasty and raw?

Stinky when dried?

Are you Good God not clean and void of all blood?

Is the spirit not void of blood? So how can we be saved with the shedding of blood?

When we shed blood do we not kill?

And take the woman's menstruation out of this now people. When we shed blood we kill hence becoming sinful. Guilty of a vile sin because we are breaking the code and or law of life and if we do this do we not sin? So how can shedding of blood be holy when it is infinitely sinful – unlawful and unholy?

When did you create death?

What does life have to do with death?

When you are dead are you not dead?

Is it not the flesh that dies in the physical and the spirit moves on? So how can someone truly die for another human being or person?

We as humans have failed Good God throughout history and now billions are going to pay with their lives. This did not have to be this way but we as humans made it so. This is our reality because I've told you lands are going to be barren. Some are going to split apart hence the judgement here on earth. Physical judgement but this is not the

final judgement. The final judgement is in the spiritual realm where all evil must die. You must serve your time in hell before you eventually die.

Right now the devil is playing for keeps because in his final hour he is going to make billions go to hell with him and he has done that already. Billions are on the docket of death but yet the belly of the beast is not yet full.

Right now the black nation is the key and he Melchesidec has us by the balls. He needs more black people in hell hence I tell you God – Good God cannot trust black people. Nor can he trust the so called Jews. Yes you white people. As a matter of fact Good God cannot trust anyone because as soon as the tide turns we are ready to bail and jump ship and many of us have and has done this. I'm ready to jump ship and I've told Good God this. I want and need to be happy but yet for some strange reason I am still in a land I truly don't want to be in and I so do not know why. He knows why but he's refusing to tell me. By him saying go South does not mean anything to me because there are many South. I need to know which Southern land to go into. If it's Lesotho, South Africa, South of France this I do not know and he Good God is not saying. But I think its South Africa that he needs me to be in but so not sure on this day. Yes I did see myself in South Africa so maybe this is where I should be. Only time will tell. And yes I am confusing you because on this day I am confused. I want to give up but can't for some strange reason. Hopefully I will get my freedom and tell you all about it.

And for the Jews and white nation that is going to take the trust statement and run don't because you are not different from the black race. ***Good God cannot trust you either hence he's never used any of you to bring forth his message.***

Yes the Israelites can say Israel is where the Jews are and they are blessed and highly favoured and I say unto them they are damned liars. ***Egypt is not Israel hence life never passed through their land. The name changing of lands do not make you holy it just makes you a damned liar – sinful.***

By saying you are from Egypt now modern day Israel does not make you a Jew it makes you a Babylonian that live in lies and deceit.

You call yourself Jews but yet write books of lies to deceive humanity then have the gaul to say you are one of Good God's own. Go back to your book of sin and truly read what

it says about you. So if you are of the Synagogue of Satan how the hell can you be the children of Good God?

You tell humanity your land is holy but yet your land is one of the unholiest no scrap that. You land is the pit of hell because you're all the devil's seed. Kill and spread lies and deceit then claim you are when you are infinitely not of Good God but of the dead.

No not all of you are false because it's only a deceitful and conniving demon that would tell lies on Good God like that and you've done all that.

You are no different from the Ethers of old, Ethiopians – Satan's children because it is though Satan that the illuminati came from. Hence you say he's the angel of light. People of the gaseous clouds is more like it hence you say Satan was an angel. Michael, Melchesidec, Aries, Zeus, Christos, Jesus, whatever name you use makes no difference, they are all death. Hence you say death procreated with humans – laid with humans to create a holy child. More like the devil's child. Oops children.

The lies that you all tell to keep Satan going is unbelievable hence the people of the world is the way we are today. Confused and hell bound.

You say Good God is your father but yet you tell lies on him. Good God was never your father; Satan is and will forever be your father because it is him that you work for. Him you lie and deceive humanity for.

BUT YOU'VE ALL FORGOTTEN THAT SATAN CANNOT GIVE YOU WHAT HE DON'T GOT.

ALL THAT HE GIVES YOU MUST BE TAKEN AWAY BECAUSE WHAT HE SATAN GIVES IS STOLEN. HE'S A THIEF HENCE MANY MILLIONAIRES AND BILLIONAIRES WILL LOSE IT ALL SHORTLY.

You cannot steal from God – Good God and don't expect to pay for your theft.

You cannot tell lies on Good God and not expect to pay for your lies.

You cannot say that Good God is with you and write lies about him to deceive humanity.

You cannot desecrate the flesh with the mark of the beast and say you are of Good God when you are not. You are going to go to hell and burn because Satan's mark is not of life it is of death. When you tattoo your skin you are accepting death. When you tattoo your eye you become sin hence eye tattoos is what our sins look like in its truest and purest form which is the spiritual form.

When you see an eye tattoo you are seeing your sins. It's that dark and ugly hence when some of us see our sins in the grave we cry like a bitch because we are seeing self – the ugliness of the sins that we did on a daily basis.

You have the truth now so live by the truth and put away wrongs.

Music is beautiful and it does heal the spirit and body. But when we have demons that sell hell to humanity Good God have to draw the line. Without good music you cannot live.

Without good music you cannot hear Good God nor sing for him because Good God uses MUSIC AS HIS COMMUNICATION TOOLS TO REACH YOU. SO WHEN YOU DISTORT THE MUSIC, HE GOOD GOD CANNOT COMMUNICATE WITH YOU.

Good God does not want or need anyone to go to hell. It is us as humans that want to go to hell and we are hell bound.

We are the ones that don't want good life hence we listen to others sell us and tell us crap – shit.

You can have your doubts about me and that's fine but like I've told you and will forever tell you. I don't want or need your soul because mine is secure with Good God. I need you to secure your soul so that when the harvest fully hits you are saved.

I don't want or need your money on earth or in the spiritual realm; I need Good God's money all around because what he gives is well given – good and true. Yes infinitely honest and good – true.

Yes you buy these books hence Good God knows my true and good heart and spirit including true love when it comes to giving back to him and his people.

Listen I refuse to do to get. Meaning I refuse to do good just for Good God to bless me. I truly love to help – do good hence I don't do to get. I cannot do it because Good God does not do to get. He does because of truth and true love. And despite my doubtful ways with him he does care about you. If he did not he would not be trying to save you with these books.

YES I BLAME HIM FOR MANY THINGS BUT WE AS HUMANS HAVE TO TAKE THE BLAME AS WELL.

I know the message. He loves us so but I need to hear I truly love you. Yes I know Good God truly loves us but I have to get down on him with the love us so business.

Off course again but this is me.

Music was given to humanity clean and like I said, music is life and if we distort music we cannot live clean. Nor can we have a good life because Good God uses music to communicate with his people.

Most of these artists don't know just how blessed they are. Some have the most beautiful of voice but yet they sell us crap. Take that beauty that Good God has and have given you and create a positive and powerful life and universe. Good God does listen to good music come on now.

It's not everyone that can write books people. Some write songs and some pray but I do not like prayers because prayers are dirty. Meaning when unclean people pray for you, you become dirty and in truth the spirit does not like prayers well my spirit anyways. It's like when I pray my brain is being distorted – runs wild that my prayer or thoughts become confusing. By the end of the prayer my thoughts would be way out in left field. How I started is not how I end and how I end is not how I started. Weird I know. And don't be confused. I started out talking to Good God and end up not talking to God but thinking about something totally different hence I start with Good God but cannot end with him hence my end is not how I started. And yes you can say I will never end with Good God because in prayer and thought Good God has no end. You will always start with him but cannot end with him because goodness and truth hath no end and this is why my thoughts are way out there.

Yes these things I know but I have to tell you them because like I said, I am no different from you. And if I've confused you with above I am sorry. Didn't mean to but by now you must know that I speak like I write and I am not your traditional or typical writer or author.

I do not have an editor or ghost writer people so bare with me. All that is written and edited is done by me. Sometimes I miss things but it cannot be helped because I try to catch all the mistakes but somehow end up failing.

These are our final day's people and like I said. Good God cannot continue to provide a home for sin because he too is sinning. When he continues to do this, provide a home for sin's children he is causing his children – people pain. He too is contributing to the root of the problem which is evil.

The devil's children cannot continue to destroy the earth and take what does not belong to them.

Because of our unclean ways Good God had to leave us but it's not all of humanity that are unclean. You still have many good people left and it is these good people that I am concerned about. It is these good people that Good God is concerned about. They are the ones that he must save. He Good God cannot save evil's children nor provide food and shelter including water for them anymore. Hence I told you about the barren lands. Shortly this must happen because the heat is not going to come from above it is going to come from the ground of the earth. Once this happens you cannot farm. No one can till the ground hence nothing will grow. Many are going to starve to death. This is the reality of man shortly hence Good God's or God's children must start preparing for the harvest to come. We have to set our houses and finances in order lest we won't make it.

You will not have water and I've told you this above.

Like I've said, the man with the food and water will become the richest person on the face of the planet. Food and water is going to become scarce and this is the reality of man – humanity because we made it so. ***WE SINNED HENCE WE ARE GOING TO GET PAID AND THAT PAY IS DEATH BECAUSE THE "WAGES OF SIN IS DEATH."***

"TRUTH IS LIFE EVERLASTING," but time and time again we choose death over life.

We know the truth but instead of living by the truth we live by lies which are our sins. So because of this we die. Death must collect his pay with the lives of humans. Like I've told you, if we sin not death cannot collect his pay. If we sin and death does not want you, meaning not ready for you, he can and will take your family member in lieu of you. ***If you have children and deal in death then your children belongs to death.***

If you signed a pact with death then your children belong to death and there are no ands ifs or buts about this. You cannot reclaim them from death because you belong to death.

I don't know how death will release your child because like I said what belongs to death he keeps. This is why it is important to choose the right partner and have children with them. Like I've told you evil pulls and it has a greater pull than good. Good does not pull hence in all that good tries to do good tries to avoid and repel all facets of evil.

Good does not want to be amongst unclean hence you will not find Good God amongst us because we are unclean.

This is why I tell Good God that he is not fair because sin and death does not play on a level playing field.

Death plays for keeps and he does keep because there is no givesy backsy with him. Hence no one can die to save another human being. Death hath no life but life hath life because life is what Good God gave us. He never ever gave us death. He gave us life and we are the ones to sign our lives over to death by accepting the lies of death's children including the clergy.

KNOW THIS. A TRUE JEW CANNOT LIE BECAUSE WE KNOW THE TRUTH OF GOOD GOD AND IT IS THE TRUTH OF GOOD GOD THAT WE MUST LIVE BY.

We cannot give you false hope nor can we give you false teachings hence I tell you and show you what I see.

I refuse to be like everyone else that say you have to go to church to find God. You can't find God in any church. You can only find death because the church is the cross of death. Hence you have the cross of death atop them and in them. And yes you wear the cross of death because some of you wear death around your neck like a noose.

We are crosses hence cross ourselves instead of letting go of the cross.

The cross killed your god but yet you go into the same place that killed your god to die. Go figure.

You didn't like your god then. Death took his life by crucifying his lying ass on a cross and now you are in the churches of death paying death for the killings he did. Death killed your god and you are still praying death and giving him your hard earned money. So what you are telling me is that you are grateful to death for killing your god.

You are grateful to death for relieving you of your pain.

Hence none of you can be faithful to Good God from what you are doing to your dead god.

Wow like I said, the full truth must be known and billions of you are in hell, meaning your name is in death's book and don't even know it.

Oh let's not forget. To top of the lies and farce of death you have his children telling you, if you kill you are going to go directly to paradise.

Tell the people you heathens that your paradise is hell, spiritual hell fire then eventual death.

Tell people Islam is a spiritual prison that once you get there you are going to burn worse than a bitch in heat. In this case the bitch is Satan.

DAMN LIARS BECAUSE EVEN GOD – GOOD GOD'S CHILDREN KNOW THE LAW THAT THOU SHALT NOT KILL IN THE PHYSICAL AND SPIRITUAL.

So how the hell can anyone say that when you kill you go automatically to paradise? Oh yea I forgot, hell is your paradise and this cannot change hence you kill to go to hell. Plain and straight you are the devil's seed.

OTHER BOOKS BY MICHELLE JEAN

Blackman Redemption – The Fall of Michelle Jean
Blackman Redemption – After the Fall Apology
Blackman Redemption – World Cry – Christine Lewis
Blackman Redemption
Blackman Redemption – The Rise and Fall of Jamaica
Blackman Redemption – The War of Israel
Blackman Redemption – The Way I Speak to God
Blackman Redemption – A Little Talk With Man
Blackman Redemption – The Den of Thieves
Blackman Redemption – The Death of Jamaica
Blackman Redemption – Happy Mother's Day
Blackman Redemption – The Death of Faith
Blackman Redemption – The War of Religion
Blackman Redemption – The Death of Russia

The New Book of Life
The New Book of Life – A Cry For The Children
The New Book of Life – Judgement
The New Book of Life – Love Bound
The New Book of Life - Me

Just One of Those Days
Book Two – Just One of Those Days
Just One of Those Days – Book Three The Way I Feel
Just One of Those Days – Book Four

The Days I Am Weak
Crazy Thoughts – My Book of Sin
Broken
Ode to Mr. Dean Fraser
A Little Little Talk

Prayers
My Collective
A Little Talk/A Time For Fun and Play
Simple Poems
Behind The Scars
Songs of Praise And Love

Love Bound
Love Bound – Book Two

Dedication Unto My Kids
More Talk
Saving America From A Woman's Perspective
My Collective the Other Side of Me
My Collective the Dark Side of Me
A Blessed Day
Lose To Win
My Doubtful Days – Book One

My Little Talk With God
My Little Talk With God – Book Two

A Different Mood and World – Thinking

My Nagging Day
My Nagging Day – Book Two

Friday September 13, 2013
My True Love
It Would Be You
My Day